100

Handpicked

Quotes

to

Know and Grow

Volume Two

Ron A. Schaefer

Cover design: Getcovers.com

This book is designed to inspire and encourage personal growth through the power of thoughtful quotes. The insights and examples shared are for general informational purposes only, with the understanding that neither the author nor the publisher is engaged in providing legal, financial, medical or other professional advice. If you seek specific guidance in legal, accounting, or financial matters, please consult a qualified professional.

A Note on Style: Although I've put great care into the content of this book, I chose not to strictly follow formal grammar and style rules, such as those outlined in *The Chicago Manual of Style*.

Quotations are anonymous unless otherwise specified.

ISBN 979-8-9913887-2-6
Library of Congress Control Number 2024917494
First Edition Published in October 2025

"We are our habits."
— Ron A. Schaefer

It's what you do every day that counts.

***

"When you discover better, you will do better."
—Inspired by the wisdom of Maya Angelou and Jim Rohn

***

Listening builds trust.

***

The cheaper you can live, the greater your options.

***

Time in the market beats timing the market.

This is especially true when it comes to long-term investing in stocks or real estate.

***

Vision without action is a daydream.
Action without vision is a nightmare.
— Attributed to a Japanese proverb

***

"Restlessness and discontent are necessities for progress."
— Thomas A. Edison (1847–1931)

Sometimes we have to hit bottom before we decide to redouble our efforts to change.

***

"The A players are constantly thinking about their to-do lists."
— Ron A. Schaefer

***

"Focus is visualizing the image you want to accomplish and keeping that image in your mind until it is done."
— Ron A. Schaefer

The more often you envision what you want to achieve, the more effort you'll make to get there.

***

"Be so good they can't ignore you."
— Steve Martin, comedian

When you're the best, people will come looking for you.

***

Long-term consistency trumps short-term intensity.
— Attributed to Bruce Lee

A New Year's resolution is not achieved in one day.

***

If you can remember why you started, then you will know why you must continue.
— Attributed to Chris Burkmenn, Nashville YouTuber

You will face setbacks, roadblocks, and negative people — own your dream.

***

"Don't use downtime as a hammock; use it as a springboard."
— Ron A. Schaefer

***

"Everything comes to him who hustles while he waits."
— Thomas A. Edison (1847–1931)

Turn waiting into winning:
- While driving, use audio learning.
- At a bus stop, use a self-study course.
- In the bathroom, read.

Work on your dream while you're waiting.

***

"Learn from the mistakes of others. You can't live long enough to make them all yourself."
— Eleanor Roosevelt

In the same way, gain wisdom from the words of others in their quotes.

**

All it takes is one good idea to save you years of hard work.

**

"Tough times don't last, tough people do."

— Robert H. Schuller, Tough *Times Never Last, But Tough People Do!* (1984)

***

"Learning is when new knowledge produces different actions."

— Ron A. Schaefer

***

"Progress is impossible without change, and those who cannot change their minds cannot change anything."
— George Bernard Shaw (1856–1950)

***

"Change your thoughts and you'll change your world."
— Norman Vincent Peale (1898–1993), American clergyman and author

***

"Nurture your mind with great thoughts, for you will never go any higher than you think."
— Benjamin Disraeli (1804–1881)

***

A centuries-old parable about sharing information uses three filters that can apply to what you choose to read or watch:
First, is what you're about to read or watch true?
Second, is this information good or kind?
Third, is the information useful?

***

"We start life with our parents' habits and either continue them or develop new ones."
— Ron A. Schaefer

***

Adapt what is useful, reject what is useless, and add what is specifically your own.
— Attributed to Bruce Lee

***

We first make our habits, and then our habits make us.

***

"People do not decide their future, they decide their habits and their habits decide their future."
— F. Matthias Alexander (1869–1955)

***

"Good habits may be more important than IQ"
— Warren Buffett, chairperson of Berkshire Hathaway

***

"Everything you want is on the other side of fear."

– George Addair (1931–2012)

What we want is on the other side of our *biggest* fears.

***

"Inaction breeds doubt and fear. Action breeds confidence and courage."

— Dale Carnegie (1888–1955)

***

"Knowing what must be done does away with fear."
— Rosa Parks (1913–2005), American civil rights activist

***

Successful people experience fear, doubt, and worry—just like everyone else. The difference is, they refuse to let those feelings hold them back.
— Inspired by T. Harv Eker, *Secrets of the Millionaire Mind*

***

"Success consists of going from failure to failure without loss of enthusiasm."
— Winston Churchill (1874–1965), Prime Minister of the United Kingdom

***

Nothing in this world can take the place of persistence.
— Attributed to Calvin Coolidge

Success is more about persistence than talent.

***

"Too many people are thinking security rather than opportunity."
— James F Byrnes (1882–1972), Former Governor of South Carolina

***

"Don't just get a job—work in a business you'd want to own. The more you learn, the more valuable you become."
— Ron A. Schaefer

***

"Money comes in slowly and goes out fast."

— Ron A. Schaefer

***

Comedian Jay Leno always had two jobs. **He'd live on the smaller income and save the big income.**

***

"You can be young without money, but you cannot be old without it."
— Tennessee Williams (1911–1983), American playwright and screenwriter

***

"In your checking account, maintain double the balance of your largest bill."
— Ron A. Schaefer

For example, if your monthly rent is $1,000, then keep $2,000 in that account, and you'll sleep better.

***

Slowlaners aim to minimize expenses; Fastlaners pursue maximum income and growing asset value.
— Attributed to M.J. DeMarco, in *the Millionaire Fastlane*

It's about managing your focus:
Focus on frugality by doing it yourself, potentially missing out on crucial information and giving up earning more money.
Focus on wealth by networking, getting a mentor, creating new revenue streams with books, annuities, businesses, and making money while you sleep.

***

"In your area, get referrals and build a network list: attorney, car repair, car detailing, doctor, drywall, electricians, financial advisors, general contractor, handyman, insurance agent, tax accountant, tile worker, etc. The honest ones will make recommendations even if they can't make a dime."
— Ron A. Schaefer

***

"First is making money.
Second is saving money (ready
cash).
Third is spending money."
— Ron A. Schaefer

✳✳✳

"Ready cash beats paid-off bills."
— Ron A. Schaefer

If you have a choice, it feels great to pay off a bill, but it's terrifying to face unemployment or an unexpected repair bill when you have to borrow money at 21 percent interest. Keep cash ready.

✳✳✳

"A man with a surplus can control circumstances, but a man without a surplus is controlled by them, and often he has no opportunity to exercise judgment."
— Harvey S. Firestone (1868–1938)

***

"Do not let a year pass by without putting money into savings or retirement."
— Ron A. Schaefer

***

"Invest $50 a day at 10 percent annual growth; in 20 years, you'll have $1 million."

— *CNBC Make It,* "Wealth Managers: Use this simple formula to retire with $1 million in 20 years." May 13, 2019

By the numbers:
$25/day in 25 years = $1 million
$10/day in 34 years = $1 million
$5/day in 41 years = $1 million

Start saving what you can:
1 percent, 5 percent, or 10 percent of money coming in. Getting started is the key. Making it a habit is life changing.

***

"Fully fund your retirement before you help your kids pay their bills."
— Ron A. Schaefer

Just like the airline safety advice *to put on your own mask first before helping others*, this quote reminds us that to secure your own financial future first.

The first way to gain time is to stop doing.

- Stop saying yes to everything.
- Stop worrying about things outside your control.
- Stop complaining.
- Stop mindless scrolling.
- Have customers build your database (i.e., do the input).
- Hire others to do small tasks or tasks you don't want to do.
- Reduce the scope of the project to the 20 percent required and eliminate the other 80 percent.

***

The Pareto 80/20 Principle comes from an Italian economist who observed in the early twentieth century that 80 percent of Italy's wealth was owned by 20 percent of the population.

Apply 80/20 to other areas:
Wardrobe: 80 percent of the time, I wear the same 20 percent of my clothing.
Sales: 80 percent of sales come from 20 percent of the products available.

Look for the 20 percent and eliminate the 80 percent time and money wasters.

***

Don't spend $1 worth of time on a 10-cent decision.

***

Know your hourly rate before choosing which tasks to work on.
— Inspired by Brian Tracy *Great Little Book on Mastering Your Time* (1997)

A desired annual salary of $100,000 ÷ 2,000 hours = $50 per hour. Only work on tasks at or above that rate and delegate or delete everything else.

***

Eisenhower Decision Matrix

	URGENT	NOT URGENT	VALUE	PEOPLE
			$$$$$	LOTS
IMPORTANT	**#1** DO	**#3** PLAN	| | | | |	| | | | |
NOT IMPORTANT	**#2** DELEGATE	**#4** DELETE	| | | | V	| | | | V
			$$	ONE

— Inspired by Dwight D. Eisenhower (1890–1969), thirty-fourth president of the United States

Note: Ron A. Schaefer added the 'value' and 'people' lines to the original matrix.

***

"Only words travel through the centuries of time."

— Ron A. Schaefer

***

"Let the people know the truth and the country is safe."

— Abraham Lincoln (1809–1865), sixteenth president of the United States

Truth results in better decisions, stability, and unification of *We the People.*

***

"Power tends to corrupt, and absolute power corrupts absolutely."
— John Emerich Edward Dalberg-Acton (1834–1902)

***

"Character is the only secure foundation of the state."
— Calvin Coolidge (1872–1933), "Speech at a New York City Lincoln Day Dinner," February 12, 1924

A nation's true strength lies in the honesty and integrity of its people.

***

"Convince a man against his will, he's of the same opinion still."
— Mary Wollstonecraft (1759–1797), *A Vindication of the Rights of Woman* (1792)

***

"Those who make peaceful revolution impossible will make violent revolution inevitable."
— John F Kennedy (1917–1963), thirty-fifth president of the United States

***

"Freedom is achieved when courage rises above fear."

— Ron A. Schaefer

***

"The proper function of government is to make it easy for the people to do good, and difficult for them to do evil."

— William Ewart Gladstone (1809–1898), British statesman and prime minister

***

"The government is us; we are the government, you and I."

—Theodore Roosevelt, twenty-sixth president of the United States.

***

"You manage things, but you lead people."

—Grace Murray Hopper (1902–1996), US Navy Admiral, American computer scientist and mathematician

***

**"A mentor who inspires one person changes a life.
A mentor who inspires other mentors shapes future generations."**
— Ron A. Schaefer

***

"We praise in public, but we correct in private."
— Vince Lombardi (1913–1970), American professional football coach

***

"What people say behind your back is your standing in the community."
— Edgar Watson Howe (1853–1937)

***

"Tone determines response."
— Ron A. Schaefer

***

"Agreeing on priorities first beats constant conflicts."
— Ron A. Schaefer

***

"Ask the tough questions up front to save time."
— Ron A. Schaefer

***

The person who knows *how* will have a job. The person who knows *why* will be the boss.
— Attributed to Diane Ravitch, an American education historian

***

"Planning is more important than knowledge. Spend more time planning than acquiring knowledge."
— Ron A. Schaefer

***

A wise man knows everything.
A shrewd one knows everyone.

***

Knowledgeable people know facts. Successful and prosperous people know people.

***

"Would you persuade, speak of interest, not of reason."
— Benjamin Franklin (1706–1790)

To be persuasive, tell the person the benefits they'll receive.

***

"No problem can withstand the assault of sustained thinking."
— Voltaire

Problems cannot withstand the bombardment of persistent thought.

***

"Any obstacle or problem we have is due to a lack of an idea."
— Ken Hakuta, American businessman, inventor, and television personality

A problem persists not because it is unsolvable, but because we have yet to think about it in a new way.

***

"The best way to a good idea is to have lots of ideas."
— Linus Pauling (1901–1994), American chemist, peace activist, and two-time Nobel Prize winner

***

"Break tasks down into smaller bites; a feast is finished one bite at a time."
— Ron A. Schaefer

***

**"Write down your dreams.
Turn them into goals.
Turn your goals into tasks.
Turn your tasks into steps."**
— Lorrin L. Lee, marketing executive

***

"First, picture your future.
Second, list the habits required
to get you to that future.
Third, focus every day on doing
those habits."
— Ron A. Schaefer

***

Tasks fall into:
   1. Must do
   2. Should do
   3. Could do

***

Five years from now, when I look back, will I see this was the right decision?

***

"Successful people have a Plan A, Plan B, and Plan C to increase their chances of success."
— Ron A. Schaefer

***

"It is better to have a fence at the edge of a cliff than to have an ambulance waiting at the bottom of the cliff."
— Joseph Malins, from the poem "A Fence or an Ambulance" (1895)

Prevention is more effective than detection and correction.

***

**Responsibility looks forward.
Blame looks backward.**

Focus your best efforts on future opportunities rather than dwelling on the past.

***

"Never look back unless you are planning to go that way."
— Henry David Thoreau (1817–1862)

***

"It's not *what* you think about, but *when*—past, present, or future."
— Ron A. Schaefer

***

"After preparing over 15,000 financial reports, I've noticed **people who struggle financially put financial decisions last as a priority, while people who build wealth spend most of their time on planning and creating their future.**"
— Ron A. Schaefer

***

**"Why grandparents say yes:
I would rather see kids try and
fail than not try at all."**
— Ron A. Schaefer

Safety comes first, but never take away an opportunity to let them figure it out, even if you know the answer.

***

One way you can often do more for your child is to do less.
— Attributed to Dr. Heather Wittenberg

***

"One father is more than a hundred schoolmasters."

— George Herbert (1593–1633)

***

"Correction does much, but encouragement does much more."

— Johann Wolfgang Von Goethe (1749–1832)

Encouragement gives us the strength to overcome any mistakes we make.

***

"Have confidence that if you have done a little thing well, you can do a bigger thing well too."
— David Storey (1933–2017), British playwright and novelist

A person is grown up, not when they can take care of themselves, but when they can take care of others.

***

"Never stomp on someone else's dream—even if you've been there and done that."
— Ron A. Schaefer

People remember how you make them feel. Kindness is more important than being right.

***

Being happy doesn't mean everything is perfect. It means you've decided to look beyond imperfection.

***

"Happiness is the only thing that multiplies when you share it."
— Albert Schweitzer

***

"After each event, look back at the emotional highs and lows and ask two questions:
1. What went well?
2. What would I do differently?"
— Ron A. Schaefer

***

"Don't rely on your memory; keep a journal. Look for yesterday's emotional highs and lows and journal only those thoughts you want to re-live that are true, kind, and useful."
— Ron A. Schaefer

***

"Dedicate your first hour each morning to self-improvement."
— Ron A. Schaefer

Your first hour sets the tone for your entire day. Use it wisely—read, exercise, journal, plan, visualize, pray, or learn something new.

***

You will never always be motivated. You will have to learn to be disciplined.

***

"It is not the mountain we conquer but ourselves."
— Sir Edmund Hillary (1919–2008), the first person to reach the summit of Mount Everest

The true victory lies within us— life's hardships shape and strengthen our character.

***

"Our priorities = our habits."
— Ron A. Schaefer

Take action: Change the order of your priorities to change your world.

***

The best investment you'll ever make … is in you.

If you enjoyed this collection, you might also love *100 Handpicked Quotes to Know and Grow, Volume 1* — the book that started it all. Discover even more timeless quotes and reflections carefully chosen to inspire, challenge, and uplift.

Find your next idea to spark change — start with Volume 1 today!